CACTI

BARELY NEED WATER!

By Tayler Cole

Gareth Stevens
PUBLISHING

Please visit our website, www.garethstevens.com. For a free color catalog of all our high-quality books, call toll free 1-800-542-2595 or fax 1-877-542-2596.

Cataloging-in-Publication Data

Names: Cole, Tayler.
Title: Cacti barely need water! / Tayler Cole.
Description: New York : Gareth Stevens Publishing, 2017. | Series: World's weirdest plants | Includes index.
Identifiers: ISBN 9781482456035 (pbk.) | ISBN 9781482456059 (library bound) | ISBN 9781482456042 (6 pack)
Subjects: LCSH: Cactus–Juvenile literature. | Desert plants–Juvenile literature.
Classification: LCC QK495.C11 C65 2017 | DDC 583'.56–dc23

First Edition

Published in 2017 by
Gareth Stevens Publishing
111 East 14th Street, Suite 349
New York, NY 10003

Designer: Katelyn E. Reynolds
Editor: Kristen Nelson

Photo credits: Cover, p. 1 Paul Starosta/Corbis Documentary/Getty Images; cover, pp. 1–24 (background) Conny Sjostrom/Shutterstock.com; cover, pp. 1–24 (sign elements) A Sk/Shutterstock.com; p. 5 PeterVrabel/ Shutterstock.com; p. 7 Joseph Bohlman/EyeEm/Getty Images; p. 9 silvergull/Shutterstock.com; p. 11 ItsAngela/Shutterstock.com; p. 13 Jim Richardson/National Geographic/Getty Images; p. 15 Richard Trible/Shutterstock.com; p. 17 Felix Junker/EyeEm/Getty Images; p. 19 James Zipp/Science Source/ Getty Images; p. 21 (illustration) nikiteev_konstantin/Shutterstock.com; p. 21 (photo) Rebou at German Wikipedia/Wikipedia.org.

Printed in China

CONTENTS

Cactus, Cacti 4

Cacti Characteristics 6

Ouch! Don't Touch Me! 8

Life in the Desert 10

Goodnight, Cactus! 12

Old Man of the Desert 14

Prickly Pear: Edible Cacti 16

Lifesaving Succulents 18

Missing Cacti 20

Glossary 22

For More Information 23

Index 24

Words in the glossary appear in **bold** type
the first time they are used in the text.

CACTUS, CACTI

Almost everyone has seen a cactus, but did you know over 2,000 different species, or kinds, of them exist? Cacti are odd-looking plants native to North and South America. Most famously, Mexico has the most species of cacti. These **succulents** range in size from less than an inch (2.5 cm) to 65 feet (20 m) high!

Most cacti have **adapted** to survive in hot, dry areas, but some are found on mountains, in rainforests, and even in cold regions such as Alaska!

SEEDS OF KNOWLEDGE

As you read, don't forget: The word "cactus" means one plant, and "cacti" means many plants!

Cacti are perennial plants. That means they grow for many years and can grow back in an area they've grown before.

5

CACTI CHARACTERISTICS

Cacti aren't often thirsty in the hot sun. In fact, they barely need any water! Each cactus has a thick-skinned stem or group of stems. These stems hold water for a long time and swell to make room for more water. The stems are covered with a waxy skin that helps keep the water from **evaporating**.

Cacti have a wide system of small, shallow roots that collect any rainwater that falls. In addition, some cacti have one long root called a taproot that runs deep into the ground.

SEEDS OF KNOWLEDGE

Like other green plants, cacti use sunlight, the gas carbon dioxide, and water to make food in a **process** called photosynthesis. For cacti, which have no leaves, this happens in their stem!

Cacti stems are fluted or ribbed, which means they have long raised bumps, easily seen in this picture. This feature is what allows the cactus to swell when the plant takes in more water.

7

OUCH!
DON'T TOUCH ME!

Cacti look a lot different than most plants. They don't have leaves! They have pointy parts called spines. Having spines is another way cacti hold on to water—they don't lose any through leaves! The spines grow in small clusters on top of mounds called areoles (EHR-ee-ohlz). Depending on the species, cactus spines can be short or long, soft or sharp, and straight or hooked.

Spines also offer shade from sun so the cactus doesn't overheat. The spines stop animals from eating the cactus, too!

With its spines and its areoles, a cactus can be a pretty weird-looking plant!

LIFE IN THE DESERT

Cacti can **reproduce** two ways. The first is through pollination. Each cactus may grow a flower. If it's pollinated, the flower will grow fruit with seeds inside. The seeds are spread by wind, rain, or an animal eating the fruit. Only a few of these seeds will survive to produce more cacti, though.

Some cacti can also reproduce another way that may sound pretty strange. A part of the plant can break off, grow roots, and become a new plant!

SEEDS OF KNOWLEDGE

Pollen is the fine yellow dust made by plants that's used in pollination. Pollination is the movement of pollen from one flower to another.

As this bee visits the cactus flower, it collects pollen. It might move it to another cactus flower.

GOODNIGHT, CACTUS!

Instead of sleeping, cacti spend the night breathing! To avoid the hot, dry desert air, cacti open their **stomata** at night to gather carbon dioxide when there's a lower chance of losing important water. They save this carbon dioxide until daytime to use for photosynthesis.

Some cacti also gather and store the sun's heat inside their stems. During the winter months, when nighttime temperatures get cold enough to freeze, cacti let out the heat in order to warm themselves!

At night, the air is cooler, so there's less evaporation.

13

OLD MAN OF THE DESERT

Native to the Southwest, the saguaro (suh-WAH-roh) is one of the most well-known kinds of cactus. Its tall, thick stem and curved arms are easy to spot. It can live up to 200 years!

During May and June, the saguaro grows white flowers that only open at night. They stay open until about noon the next day. If fertilized, these flowers will begin to grow fruit. In the past, this juicy fruit was an important food for Native Americans living in the desert.

SEEDS OF KNOWLEDGE

Saguaros grow very slowly, only about 1 inch (2.5 cm) per year. Very old saguaros may grow to have five arms and be 30 feet (9 m) tall!

14

PRICKLY PEAR: EDIBLE CACTI

The prickly pear cactus can grow up to 6 or 7 feet (1.8 or 2.1 m) tall. It has large, thin, round pads that branch off each other. They store water for the cactus and are covered in tiny spines called glochids (GLOH-kuhdz).

The prickly pear has yellow, red, or purple flowers. These flowers can produce fruits called tuna that are eaten all across Mexico. The pads can be eaten once the spines have been taken out carefully and they're cooked.

SEEDS OF KNOWLEDGE

The thicker the pad is on a prickly pear cactus, the older it is!

People wear gloves when they pick the fruit of the prickly pear cactus. Once glochids get in your skin, they're hard to get out!

17

LIFESAVING SUCCULENTS

A cactus is an important part of its **ecosystem**. Birds use cacti branches to build nests, taking advantage of the spines to keep the nests safe.

During their northern **migration**, bats drink the nectar of the saguaro, cardon, and organ pipe cacti. Cactus bees use pollen to feed their larvae. Desert animals also eat cacti, and birds eat their fruit. While people can eat cacti, we can only drink from one kind of barrel cactus. The liquid in most cacti would make you sick!

SEEDS OF KNOWLEDGE

Cacti don't store water in the same form as what we drink when thirsty. It has matter in it that's not safe for people to drink.

Saguaro cacti grow so tall that this nest is safe from predators!

19

MISSING CACTI

Most kinds of cacti aren't close to dying out, but the government has laws to keep them safe—just in case. Cactus populations are **threatened** by animals that step on the plants. Cactus collectors dig up certain kinds of cacti and take them home, too.

Global **climate change** can also threaten cacti and the desert ecosystem. To keep these weird plants from harm, be careful not to waste water and respect the natural world around you!

WEIRD WAYS CACTI SAVE WATER

- thick, waxy covering on stems
- fluted stems
- spines instead of leaves
- open stomata at night
- grows slowly
- shallow root system collects rain quickly
- taproot finds water deep underground

The Winkler cactus is one small cactus that's often stolen by collectors! What a strange plant—and an odd hobby!

GLOSSARY

adapt: to change to suit conditions

climate change: changes in worldwide weather patterns, including the warming of Earth and changes in rainfall and wind patterns

ecosystem: all the living things in an area

evaporate: to change from a liquid to a gas

migration: movement to warmer or colder places for a season

process: to move something forward in a set of steps. Also, the set of steps itself.

reproduce: when a living thing creates another living thing just like itself

stomata: openings in a stem or leaf that allow for gases like carbon dioxide to pass through

succulent: a plant that is able to exist in dry places by using water stored in its leaves or stems

threaten: to give signs that harm might be coming

FOR MORE INFORMATION

Books

Cohen, Marina. *Deserts Inside Out.* New York, NY: Crabtree Publishing Company, 2015.

Rae, Rowena. *Cacti.* New York, NY: Smartbook Media, Inc., 2017.

Websites

Cool Cacti, Super Succulents
society.bcss.org.uk/coolcacti/succulents.html
Find out more about all the different types of cacti around the world.

Did You Know? Cacti
bbc.co.uk/gardening/gardening_with_children/didyouknow_cacti.shtml
Click on the link at the bottom of the page and create your own cactus garden!

World Biomes: Desert
kids.nceas.ucsb.edu/biomes/desert.html
Learn more about the desert biome!

INDEX

areoles 8, 9

climate change 20

collectors 20

ecosystem 18, 20

flower 10, 14, 15, 16

fruit 10, 14, 16, 17, 18

glochids 16, 17

laws 20

Mexico 4, 16

North America 4

pads 16

photosynthesis 6, 12

pollen 10, 11, 18

pollination 10

prickly pear cactus 16, 17

roots 6, 10, 21

saguaro 14, 15, 18, 19

seeds 10

South America 4

spines 8, 9, 16, 18, 21

stem 6, 12, 14, 21

stomata 12, 21

succulents 4

taproot 6, 21

tuna 16

water 6, 7, 8, 12, 16, 18, 20, 21

waxy skin 6, 21